Finding the Right Words
for the Holidays

Also by J. Beverly Daniel

Finding the Right Words

Finding the Right Words for the Holidays

Festive Phrases to Personalize
Your Holiday Greetings & Newsletters

J. Beverly Daniel

POCKET BOOKS
New York   London   Toronto   Sydney

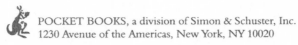 POCKET BOOKS, a division of Simon & Schuster, Inc.
1230 Avenue of the Americas, New York, NY 10020

Library of Congress Cataloging-in-Publication Data
Daniel, J. Beverly.
  Finding the right words for the holidays : festive phrases to personalize your
holiday greetings & newsletters / J. Beverly Daniel.—1st Pocket Books hardcover ed.
    p. cm
  ISBN-13: 978-1-4165-1344-5
  ISBN-10:   1-4165-1344-2
    1.Christmas cards. 2. Hanukkah. 3. Newsletters. I. Title.

NC1866.C5D35 2005
808'.066395—dc22   2005050931

This Pocket Books hardcover edition October 2005

10 9 8 7 6 5 4 3 2 1

POCKET and colophon are registered trademarks of
Simon & Schuster, Inc.

Manufactured in the United States of America

For information regarding special discounts for bulk purchases,
please contact Simon & Schuster Special Sales at 1-800-456-6798
or business@simonandschuster.com

To my granddaughter,

Molly,

who makes every holiday more fun!

Acknowledgments

I would like to send many thanks to my family: John; Eric; Tracey; George; and my granddaughter, Molly; for all their patience, understanding, and support while I was writing my book.

To my parents, Frank Hoffman and the late Mildred Hoffman, my deepest gratitude for making the holidays a joyful time and an important part of my life. To my brothers, John, Greg, and Joe, thanks for making the holidays special when we were kids.

I am grateful to my editor, Micki Nuding, for her encouragement, guidance, and continuous enthusiasm for my endeavor. It has been a joy to work with Micki.

With deep appreciation, I would like to acknowledge my

terrific agent, Mary Tahan, and also Jena Anderson of Mary M. Tahan Literary Agency. Their interest and help made my job so much easier. I not only think of Mary as my agent, but I also consider her a friend.

Special thanks to Karen Eichner and Kelly Loftus for their enthusiasm and kindness.

Also, special thanks to my good buddy, Dennis Warwick.

Contents

Introduction

'Tis the week before the holidays and I'm in a tizzy,
The shopping, the baking, the decorating—I'm dizzy!
And the holiday cards! I still haven't sent 'em,
My pen's in my hand, but the words, I can't find 'em!

If you're anything like me, you vow each year after Thanksgiving that this time, this holiday season, you're going to do things *right.* You're going to be totally organized. The decorations will be up weeks ahead of time. All the gifts will be bought and wrapped with days to spare. There'll be no last-minute run to a mob scene at Toys "R" Us; no baking cookies at midnight the night before guests arrive.

And the holiday cards? You'll write them out—thoughtfully, with personalized greetings—and mail them in plenty of time to arrive before the holidays.

Right?

Well, that's where this little book will come in handy. *Finding the Right Words for the Holidays* has everything you need to make writing holiday greeting cards a snap. Inside are how-to's for writing the Family Holiday Newsletter; helpful hints to simplify holiday card-sending; Holiday Card Recipient Lists, in which you can record the names of people to whom cards will be sent; even a list of state abbreviations. Best of all, and most important, there are lists of perfect phrases for each holiday—Christmas, Hanukkah, Kwanzaa, and the New Year—as well as famous sayings and poems. And the greetings and sayings are interchangeable: feel free to choose among them, to mix and match them as you please, especially if you're part of a family that blends together two or more traditions—Christmas and Hanukkah; or Christmas and Kwanzaa, for example.

No more sitting with pen in hand, staring into space, waiting for inspiration to strike. Simply pick up this book and *voilà!* You'll find all the right words at your fingertips.

Christmas

For many of us, Christmas is the most joyous and festive holiday of the year. Christians around the world are celebrating the birth of Christ. Midnight mass on Christmas Eve in a church lit by candlelight is the magical high point of the season for many families.

There is so much preparation that goes on before the arrival of this holiday. The weeks before are a whirlwind of shopping, wrapping gifts, decorating our homes, baking cookies, and card-sending. The Christmas season is a time to renew old friendships and acquaintances and update them on everything that has occurred during the year.

There are many traditions, legends, and lore connected with the season, the Christmas tree and mistletoe being two of the most popular.

✺ *Christmas Tree* ✺

Perhaps the most beloved and well-known symbol of Christmas is the evergreen tree strung with colored lights, garlands of popcorn, and ornaments. For many Americans, the holiday isn't complete until the tree is up and decorated. Yet less than two hundred years ago, most Americans considered the Christmas tree an oddity, even a symbol of paganism.

The origins of the holiday tree do date back to pagan times. In northern Europe, the Vikings regarded the evergreen as a symbol of life in the cold, barren winter and as the promise of the return of spring. The druids of England and France decorated oaks to honor their gods of harvest, and the Romans decorated trees during their Saturnalia festivals in December.

How did this pagan symbol become linked to the Christian celebration of the birth of Christ? There are many legends about the Christmas tree, one of which is the story of St. Boniface. He was an eighth-century English monk who worked as a missionary in Germany. There, at Geismar, was a great oak tree sacred to the thunder god, Thor. It is said that one day St. Boniface came upon a group of pagans preparing to sacrifice a child at the foot of the great oak. To save the child and stop the pagan ritual, Boniface felled the oak. Folklore has it that a small fir tree sprang up, which Boniface said represented the Tree of Life and the life of Christ. When no thunderbolt issued from Thor struck down the monk, many of the heathens converted to Christianity. Tradition has it that the fall of this oak marked the fall of heathenism.

The tradition of decorating a tree indoors at Christmas appears to have begun in Germany. German Christians would bring fir trees into their homes and decorate them with colored paper flowers, fruits, sweets, homemade cookies, and candles. Eventually the tradition spread throughout Europe. The English royalty publicly embraced the Christmas tree in 1841, when Prince Albert, husband of Queen Victoria, decorated a tree at Windsor Castle for the first time.

When German Christians immigrated to America, they brought along their Christmas traditions. One of the first public displays of a Christmas tree in America was set up by German settlers in Pennsylvania. The fourteenth president of the United States, Franklin Pierce, began the tradition of a Christmas tree in the White House in 1856, but it wasn't until the late 1800s that most Americans began to accept the Christmas tree into their homes.

Today, the president lights the national Christmas tree in Washington, D.C. All across the country, as well as throughout Europe and other parts of the world, the Christmas tree has become a cherished tradition.

🌿 Mistletoe 🌿

Hanging mistletoe in a doorway of our homes is a holiday tradition many Americans and other people around the world practice. Why do we hang a piece of shrubbery with pointy green leaves and waxy red or white berries in an archway? And why on earth do we kiss underneath it?

Mistletoe is a parasitic plant that grows on trees; its roots penetrate the tree's bark and draw nutrients from the tree. Mistletoe is poisonous; ingesting it can cause cramps, diarrhea, even death. (So if you plan to have it in the house during the holidays, be sure to keep it out of reach of children and pets.)

How did this poisonous plant get tied up with kissing and Christmas?

Ancient peoples believed the plant was related to fertility. The druids of Britain believed mistletoe could miraculously heal the sick, give fertility to humans and animals, and ward off witchcraft.

The custom of kissing under mistletoe may have come from any or all of these ancient beliefs, or it may have come from the Vikings, who associated the plant with Frigga, the goddess of love and beauty. Viking legend has it that, in the eighth century, Balder, the god of the summer sun, had a dream that he was going to die. He told his mother, Frigga, about the dream. Desperate to save her son from death, the goddess of love and beauty went to all the elements—earth, air, fire, and water—as well as all the plants and animals, and asked them not to kill her son. Nonetheless, Balder's enemy, Loki, managed to have Balder killed with a dart made of poisonous mistletoe.

For three days, all the elements tried vainly to bring Balder back to life. Finally, Frigga's tears of grief for her dead son changed the mistletoe's berries from red to white, and Balder was miraculously brought back to life. In joy and gratitude, Frigga kissed everyone who walked beneath mistletoe.

It is said that each time a man kisses a woman beneath the mistletoe, he should remove one berry. When all the berries are gone, there should be no more kissing underneath that plant. The unmarried woman who is left unkissed will remain single for another year!

✣ Christmas Phrases ✣

Wishing you the Christmas spirit all year long

May your heart be filled with every joy this lovely season brings

May the snow fall lightly and the sun shine brightly on your Christmas holiday

May the wonderful blessing of Christmas remain yours throughout the year

May the warm glow of the holiday lights reach from our home to yours

Hoping the fire in your hearth keeps you warm and toasty during this holiday season

Wishing you a heavenly Christmas

Best wishes for peace, health, and happiness

Hoping your Christmas stocking is filled to the brim with goodies

May the sights and sounds of Christmas fill your home with joy

May the spirit of Christmas bring you peace and joy

Wishing you happiness and cheer during the Christmas
season and always

All good wishes for a happy holiday season and a
prosperous New Year

Wishing you all things bright and beautiful at Christmas
and all year

Warmest holiday wishes from our home to yours

In the true spirit of the season, wishing you peace and joy

May your Christmas be blessed with peace and happiness

May love, hope, and happiness be yours at Christmas and
always

May your Christmas be blessed with much love and joy

Hope your holidays are happy days!

Wishing you peace, health, and happiness at Christmas and
always

May this season be filled with joy and delight for you and
those you love

Distance can never separate true friends during this
wonderful Christmas season

Wishing you a Christmas full of peace, happiness, love, and
light

May all the joys of Christmas light up your heart

Wishing a bright and happy holiday to you and those you
love

May the wonderful sounds of Christmas carols fill your
hearts with joy

There is always a special place in my heart for you during
this wonderful time of the year

Till I can be there in person, here's a holiday hug for you

Wishing you a healthy and happy Christmas

May your Christmas be filled with peace and harmony

Santa and I are dashing through the snow to wish you a
very Merry Christmas

May the Christmas season bring back memories of cold, snowy days and hot, steamy cocoa

Wishing you holiday fun for the whole family

May you have a wonderful and nostalgic Christmas

Hoping your Christmas is a winter wonderland

There is nothing like the fragrance of fresh pine during the holiday season

Thinking of past Christmases together and all the joys we shared

It's finally winter! Get out the skis and have a very Merry Christmas

The lights are glowing, the house is bedecked, happiness
   prevails, and I'm wishing you a very Merry Christmas

Deck the halls, trim the tree, wrap the packages, and have a
   very Merry Christmas

May there be peace in the world throughout the Christmas
   season and always

May the joy of this Christmas season remain with you now
   and always

Sending the happiest of season's greetings to our dearest
   friends

Remembering you with the warmest of wishes for a very
   Merry Christmas

Wishing you a "flurry" of Christmas good wishes

May all your Christmas moments be precious

May your Christmas be filled with many treasures and
surprises

Sending all good wishes, and may your Christmas table be
plentiful

As you gather around the Christmas table, my thoughts will
be with you

Sending much affection to you and yours during this wonderful Christmas season

Wishing you a most memorable Christmas

Sending all happy thoughts to brighten your Christmas
holiday

Wishing you a most unforgettable Christmas

Thinking of you at Christmas brings back many sweet
memories

Sending a warm embrace across the miles during this
glorious Christmas holiday

May the peace and tranquillity of the season be yours at
Christmas and all year

May your Christmas celebration be full of gentle joys

Christmas Religious Phrases

Celebrate the birth of Christ with much joy

May you rejoice in the birth of Christ on this glorious Christmas Day

May the miracle of Bethlehem inspire you

May the light of Christ shine upon you

May the Star of Bethlehem light the way to peace and happiness forever

Hoping God's blessings will be with you always

Wishing you a holy and joyous Christmas

May the blessing of the Lord's love fill your heart

May your life be enriched with Christ's blessing now and
 always

The Savior is born. Let us celebrate and rejoice!

May the wonder and joy of Jesus' birth bring us peace and
 guidance

On this glorious Christmas Day, let His light guide us

May the peace and joy of this Holy Season be with you
 always

May the tranquillity and joy of the Nativity be with you and
 your family

May the knowledge that He is born on this glorious day
 bring you peace and hope

❧ Christmas Humor ❧

I bought you a very expensive Christmas gift, but my credit
card was turned down.

I miss you so much this Christmas, but at least my
checking account has some money in it.

Santa could be in real trouble this year. His computer is
down!

I knew Santa was far too jovial . . . too much eggnog!

Broken leg? I told you not to stand on an icy roof to put up
the Christmas lights!

I went to buy your Christmas present, but the dollar store
was closed.

Santa must be a woman, because no man could accomplish all that in one night!

Please, Santa, enough with the animal-shaped pottery planters that grow grass!

Hope Santa isn't late because he had to stop to ask for directions.

Christmas must be close. Mom is cleaning the house.

The Christmas tree is decorated so beautifully, but why is it moving? Uh-oh, where's the cat?

Sending special holiday thoughts to my sweetheart. "Marry" Christmas!

We made it easier for Santa this year and greased the chimney!

I like your clever doorstop. It looks just like the fruitcake I gave you last year.

I wish someone would come up with some Christmas carols for the musically challenged!

If you're not desperate, why are you wearing mistletoe in your hair?

Christmas is that wonderful season of card giving—when we all give to MasterCard, Visa, AMEX. . . . Have a Merry Christmas!

Remember to behave at the office Christmas party. Remember what you did last year?

Who's the idiot that said Christmas isn't about presents?

I know you want to hear those wonderful three little words
   at Christmas. Okay. . . . Let's go shopping!!

I wanted to make certain Santa found our house all right, so
   I emailed him the map website.

Naughty or nice, who cares, where're my presents?

I bought you a really neat gift for Christmas this year.
   Please excuse the large box and airholes.

Like Santa says, "On Donner! On Blitzen! On Sleepy!
   Sneezy! Goofy!?!" Oh heck, you get the picture. Merry
   Christmas to all, and to all a Good Night!

Let me make this perfectly clear, Santa: I want it all, and I
   want it now!

Santa says, "Forget the milk and cookies, and make it
champagne and strawberries!"

Deck the halls with houghs of bolly . . . oops . . . too much
eggnog again. Oh well, Merry Christmas!

Santa knows you've been a good boy [girl] this year, so no
coal for you! Happy Holidays!

This holiday season, indulge, and may nothing—not
cheesecake, nor magic bars, nor chocolate bonbons—go
to your waist!

'Tis the night before Christmas and all through the house,
not a creature is stirring except me, assembling that
#$%@ bike [train, car] till the wee hours of the
morning. May you have a merry and restful holiday!

❧ Famous Christmas Quotations ❧

At Christmas I no more desire a rose
Than wish a snow in May's newfangled
   mirth;
But like of each thing that in season
   grows.

                —William Shakespeare

At Christmas play and make good cheer,
For Christmas comes but once a year.

                —Thomas Tresser

Happy Christmas to all, and to all a
   goodnight!

              —Clement Clarke Moore

'Most all the time, the whole year round,
   there ain't no flies on me,
But jest 'fore Christmas I'm as good as I
   kin be!

                      —Eugene Field

I will honor Christmas in my heart, and
   try to keep it all the year.

                      —Charles Dickens

Heap on more wood!—The wind is chill;
But let it whistle as it will,
We'll keep our Christmas merry still.

                      —Sir Walter Scott

For little children everywhere
A joyous season still we make;

We bring our precious gifts to them,
Even for the dear child Jesus' sake.

—Phoebe Cary

Christmas won't be Christmas without
    any presents.

—Louisa May Alcott

A good conscience is a continual
    Christmas.

—Benjamin Franklin

A turkey never voted for an early
    Christmas.

—Irish proverb

Hanukkah

Hanukkah means "dedication," and it's also called the Festival of Lights. In this eight-day celebration, the menorah (a nine-branched candle lamp) is nightly lit with one candle for each of the eight nights. Because this holiday follows the lunar Jewish calendar, the dates for the eight-day celebration vary from year to year, falling between November and January.

The Hanukkah story is ancient, dating back over 2,300

years to a time when the Jews were oppressed and the Temple of Jerusalem was desecrated. After three years of battle, the Jews overthrew their oppressors and reclaimed their temple. To rededicate the temple, the eternal light, which is present in every Jewish house of worship, had to be relit. Once lit, the light should never be allowed to die out. But the Jews found only a tiny bit of oil—enough to light an oil lamp for only one night. Still, the lamp was lit.

And then a wondrous thing happened. The oil lasted for eight nights, enough time for the Jews to prepare a new supply of oil. The eight-day Hanukkah celebration was born of this miracle.

Menorah

The menorah is a very important part of this beautiful celebration. A candelabrum whose original design is found in the Torah, the menorah is one of the oldest symbols of Judaism.

For the celebration of Hanukkah, it contains holders for nine candles. The center and tallest candle—known as the *shamash*—is used to light the remaining eight candles (four on each side of the *shamash*) as they are placed in their holders each night after sundown.

The candles are placed in the holders from right to left and lit each evening starting from left to right. One candle is lit on the first night, two on the second night, and so on.

✍ *Dreidel* ✍

The dreidel game is a holiday tradition especially enjoyed by children.

The dreidel is a four-sided spinning top with a Hebrew letter on each of its four sides: *nun, gimel, heh,* and *shin.* These letters mean "A Great Miracle Happened There."

In the game, these letters also mean:

nun—neither win nor lose
gimel—take all
heh—take half
shin—put in a token

The players are given a certain number of coins, pieces of candy, peanuts, chocolate, or other goodies as tokens or chips to play with. Each player puts a chip in the kitty. The players then take turns spinning the dreidel; when the top stops, the letter facing up decides the player's fate.

When a player loses all his tokens, he's out of the game. The game ends when all but the last person is out of tokens, or when everyone agrees to stop.

✎ *Hanukkah Phrases* ✐

Wishing a bright and happy Hanukkah to you and your
loved ones

Hoping this Hanukkah season finds you healthy and
happy

May your home overflow with happiness on this joyful
Hanukkah holiday

Wishing you all peace and happiness on this wonderful
family holiday

May the lighting of the Hanukkah candles bring you joy
and peace

Hoping this wondrous festival of light finds you all well
and happy

Thinking of you and your family during this glorious
eight-day celebration

Wishing you a warm and glowing Hanukkah season

Sending you the gift of love during this happy Hanukkah season

Sending many blessings from our home to yours

Wishing you everlasting peace during Hanukkah and always

With each candle lit, may your heart be warmed and your soul satisfied

May the light from the menorah shine upon you now and forever

So many happy memories of you come flooding back during the Hanukkah celebration, Grandma and Grandpa

We all join in wishing you a peaceful and happy Hanukkah

Mom and Dad, you have always made this such a happy
    season for us

May peace fill the hearts of all you love

Sending warm Hanukkah wishes to you and yours

Thinking of you during this wonderful Hanukkah season

Because of you, the traditions of Hanukkah have always
    meant so much to me

Wishing you love and laughter during this wonderful
    Hanukkah season and always

Hoping you have a Hanukkah full of love and light

May the happiness and joy of this blessed season be with
    you now and throughout the coming year

May the spirit of this holiday give you comfort and peace always

Hoping your Hanukkah celebration will be a joyful occasion for you and your family

Thinking of friends at this time of the year brings us closer together

May your Hanukkah season be filled with love, laughter, and peace

May you win all the chocolate gelt when you spin the dreidel!

There are no friends like old friends at Hanukkah and always

Thinking of special neighbors during this happy Hanukkah holiday

As the snow falls gently from above, I wish you a very
    happy Hanukkah

Hoping you are enjoying the peace and tranquillity of this
    wonderful holiday

Happy Hanukkah to very special people in my life

Sending much love and affection during this wonderful
    Hanukkah season

As your family gathers for this wonderful holiday, my heart
    will be with you

May all your hopes and dreams come true during this
    wonderful Hanukkah holiday

Wishing you a plentiful holiday table and happiness
    always

Sending wholehearted wishes for a glorious Hanukkah

Wishing you and your loved ones good fortune and
happiness during the Hanukkah season

Sending many greetings across the miles for a very Happy
Hanukkah

The Hanukkah celebration won't be the same without
you

Sending my deepest affection and sincerest wishes for a
Happy Hanukkah

Sending warmest regards for a very Happy Hanukkah
season

Hoping you have a delightful Hanukkah

Wishing you peace and harmony during the wonderful
   holiday season

Sending an abundance of good wishes for a very Happy
   Hanukkah

May the luminous lights of the Hanukkah candles find you
   all healthy and happy

Wishing you a perfect and Happy Hanukkah

Sending you a warm embrace during this Hanukkah
   season

Wishing you prosperity and joy and a very Happy
   Hanukkah

Sending compliments of the season to you and yours

May the magic of the holiday season be yours

Hoping your holiday season is filled with many gentle joys

We are all thinking of you and sending best wishes for a
Happy Hanukkah

May blessings shower down on your near and dear ones on
this happy Hanukkah

May your Hanukkah be filled with new hopes and joy

May the beauty of the Hanukkah season be with you all
year

You are always close to my heart, but especially at this time
of the year

Hoping these Hanukkah wishes brighten your day

May the glow from the Hanukkah candles light up your heart

Sending the gift of love and peace at this happy Hanukkah season

✤ Hanukkah Religious Hebrew Phrases ✤

Nes gadol haya—A great miracle happened there

Baruch Atah Adonai Elohaynu, Melech Ha Olam—Blessed are you, Lord Our God, King of the world

Baruch Hashem Adonai—Blessed be the Name of the Lord

Hodu L'Adonai Ki Tov—Give thanks to the Lord

Chag Same'ach—Happy Holiday

Am Yisrael Chai—Israel lives and our people live

Hari'u La Adonai—Make a joyful noise to the Lord

Shalom Aleichem—Peace be on you

Shalom Aleichem B'Shem HaMelekh—Peace be upon you in the Name of the King

Sha-alu Shalom Yerushalayim—Pray for the peace of Jerusalem

Todah La'el—Thanks be to God

Hashem Ro'l—The Lord is my Shepherd

Kadosh Adonai Eloheynu—The Lord Our God is holy

Melo Kil Ha'aretz Kevod—The whole earth is full of His glory

Ve'ahavat Olam Ahavtich—Yea, I have loved thee with an everlasting love (Jer 31:3)

❧ *Hanukkah Humor* ☙

One good thing about Hanukkah is that we never have to clean up the lawn after flying reindeer

Forget the fruitcake, give us the chocolate gelt

Hanukkah means you never have to clean your fireplace before the holiday

Eight days of presents are much better than one

Home is where the heart is at Hanukkah, unless you're on the cleanup committee

Happy Hannukah . . . um, Happy Chanukah . . . um, Happy Hanukkah, oh well . . . Happy Holiday

Remember to keep the cat away from the lit menorah!

If I kvetch more, will I get more presents?

At Hanukkah you can be naughty or nice and still get presents

Never come empty-handed to a Hanukkah celebration!

Without you, the Hanukkah celebration is like chicken soup without matzo balls

I sure hope I get a practical gift for Hanukkah, like a sports car or a trip to Hawaii

Did anyone stop at the doughnut shop to get the jelly
doughnuts?

Who put the joke candles in the menorah?

When you get a Hanukkah gift, you have seven days to
exchange it

No cheating during the dreidel game!

At least you don't have to buy Hanukkah seals

It's cheaper to mail blintzes than fruitcake. (And they taste
better!)

At least we don't have to decorate the menorah with tinsel
and ornaments

Thank heavens Chinese restaurants are open on Christmas
Eve

Okay, who used the *shamash* when the electricity went out?

No more stress—next year we're spending the holiday on a beach!

I'm starting my own Hanukkah tradition this year. Shop till you drop!

One thing for certain, don't start your diet until after Hanukkah

I'd like to light the menorah this year, but my mother told me not to play with matches

Kwanzaa

Kwanzaa is an African-American and Pan-African holiday that celebrates community, culture, and family. A relatively new holiday, it was created in 1966 by Dr. Maulana Karenga, professor of black studies at California State University, Long Beach.

Though this holiday is less than forty years old, its roots reach back centuries. Kwanzaa comes from *matunda ya kwanza,* a phrase in Swahili—the most widely spoken African language—meaning "first fruits of the harvest." In African history, peoples of ancient Egypt, Nubia, Ashantiland, and Yorubaland held first-fruits celebrations. These celebrations are also found in modern times (as well as ancient) among the Zulu in Swaziland, and the Matabele, Thonga, and Lovedu of southeastern Africa.

Kwanzaa builds on the five fundamental activities of traditional continental African first-fruit celebrations:

- *Ingathering—the reaffirmation of the bonds among people*
- *Reverence—the giving of thanks to the creator for the blessings of creation*
- *Commemoration—the payment of honor to one's ancestors and past*
- *Recommitment—the vow to uphold the best of African cultural thought and practice, and*
- *Celebration—the celebration of life and existence, family, community, and culture*

Kwanzaa is a seven-day celebration, beginning on December 26 and ending on New Year's Day, January 1. Each of the seven days is dedicated to one of the following seven principles: unity, self-determination, collective work and responsibility, cooperative economics, purpose, creativity, and faith.

The traditional colors of Kwanzaa are black, red, and green—black for the people, red for their struggle, and green for the future. The central ritual is the lighting of the kinara, a candelabrum with seven candles. There is one black candle in the center; three red candles to the left, and three green candles to the right. At each evening meal during Kwanzaa, members of the family light one candle. On the first night, the black candle in the center representing unity is lit. The remaining candles—the three red candles representing self-determination, cooperative economics, and creativity, and the three green candles of collective work, purpose, and faith— are lit from left to right on the following evenings.

Black, red, and green are also used to decorate the house

for this holiday, as are African art objects, baskets, and woven fabrics.

Today, more than twenty million people around the world celebrate this holiday. Being neither a political nor religious holiday, Kwanzaa can be practiced alongside the religious celebration of your choice.

Kwanzaa Phrases

May your home be aglow with the spirit of Kwanzaa

Let us sow the seeds of dedication to this holiday and harvest the peace that follows

Sending you the warmest of Kwanzaa wishes

As we light the Kwanzaa candles, let it remind us of our heritage

May the spirit of Kwanzaa be in your heart always

May the unity and love of this holiday bring us all closer
together

Wishing you unity and love on this joyous occasion

Hoping this Kwanzaa holiday means a new beginning for
you and your loved ones

May the lighting of the candles illuminate the pride you feel

Thinking of you during Kwanzaa and always

May the lighting of the candles light up your heart

Thinking of the Kwanzaa feast brings back many happy
memories

We are sending the glow of happiness from our home to yours

Wishing you love and warmth to make this Kwanzaa season special

May the strength of our convictions bring us all closer together

May the Kwanzaa holiday find you and your family well and happy

I am sending you good wishes during this happy season because you are very special to me

May your Kwanzaa celebration bring you closer to your history and heritage

Wishing you peace and prosperity during this Kwanzaa
   holiday and always

Though I cannot be with you during this wonderful
   Kwanzaa celebration, I will be there in mind and spirit

Hoping you celebrate the Kwanzaa holiday with honor and
   pride

Best wishes for peace, health, and happiness on this holiday

May you find inspiration and love during this happy season

Warmest wishes from our home to yours during this
   holiday season and always

May you and your family have a bountiful Kwanzaa holiday

In the true spirit of the Kwanzaa celebration, wishing you peace and joy

May the peace and unity you share at this time last forever

Wishing all the best to you and yours during Kwanzaa and all year long

Have faith and believe in yourself, and happiness will follow

Sending warmest wishes from our home to yours

This is the season for pride and commitment for us and those we love

This happy Kwanzaa holiday means even more when you can share it with friends

May this time of celebration and reflection be a treasured
   memory always

May your Kwanzaa celebration be a memorable one

There is no place like home for the holiday season

Enjoy the holiday and preserve your family traditions

May you weave the origins and traditions of the Kwanzaa
   holiday into your daily life

May your Kwanzaa holiday be full of special delights

Thinking of special neighbors during this joyous holiday

May you and your family find happiness and great joy
   through the traditions of Kwanzaa

Hoping your Kwanzaa holiday is full of friends, family, and fun

May your Kwanzaa table be plentiful

Sending wholehearted wishes for a great Kwanzaa celebration

As you and your family gather together during this wonderful holiday, my heart will be with you

Missing you and sending you warm regards at this joyful time

May this wonderful Kwanzaa holiday turn special moments into happy memories

May all your joys be plentiful at Kwanzaa and always

Sending wholehearted wishes for a happy Kwanzaa

Wishing you happiness and good fortune at Kwanzaa and
always

As you join hands around the Kwanzaa table, may the peace
of the season be yours

Wishing you a delightful Kwanzaa celebration

Sending sincere wishes for a very special Kwanzaa

Hoping your Kwanzaa holiday is a most memorable one

Sending warmest regards for a very happy Kwanzaa

May your Kwanzaa celebration sparkle with all the
festivities

Hoping you have a delightful Kwanzaa celebration

Wishing you harmony and happiness at Kwanzaa and always

May you have a marvelous Kwanzaa

Remembering previous Kwanzaa celebrations, and missing
you very much

As you observe this happy holiday, keep me in your
thoughts

Wishing you an abundance of happiness and good fortune
during the Kwanzaa holiday

Sending a warm embrace to all across the miles

May the Kwanzaa candles brighten your Kwanzaa
celebration

Wishing you a perfect and happy Kwanzaa

May this be one of your most memorable Kwanzaa
celebrations ever

Hoping your Kwanzaa celebration leaves you with many
sweet memories

May you have a dazzling Kwanzaa holiday

Harambee!—Let's all pull together (Swahili)

Wishing you peace and tranquillity during this wonderful
holiday

Sending an abundance of happy wishes for your Kwanzaa
celebration

Thinking of you at this wonderful time of the year and
wishing you a happy Kwanzaa

Wishing you all the best at this festive time of the year

This Kwanzaa holiday brings back many happy memories

May the magic of this holiday season be yours now and always

Hoping this Kwanzaa holiday is filled with gentle joys

May this festive season find you all healthy and happy

Many happy wishes for a joyous holiday season

Wishing you love and peace at Kwanzaa and always

Family traditions mean so much all year, but especially
during Kwanzaa

May your home be full of fun, love, and laughter during
the Kwanzaa celebration

Sending hugs across the miles for Kwanzaa

Wishing you peace, joy, and happiness at Kwanzaa and always

Sending good wishes from our family to yours at Kwanzaa
and always

May this wonderful holiday bring you everything bright
and beautiful

Wishing you all the pleasures of a very happy Kwanzaa

Hoping your Kwanzaa is filled with new hopes and much joy

May this wonderful Kwanzaa holiday fill you with hope and
inspiration

You are close to my heart at Kwanzaa and always

Wishing you and your family a most joyous Kwanzaa

Your friendship is a gift to treasure at Kwanzaa and always

❧ *Kwanzaa Humor* ☙

I can hardly wait for the Kwanzaa feast. Is it all right if I
    invited twenty of my closest friends?

The shortest distance between two points during Kwanzaa
    is between my house and yours

Keeping in mind the principle of unity, there will be no
    arguments on Kwanzaa about the last piece of cake—it's
    mine!

"Collective work and responsibility" means you get to do
   the dishes

For my Kwanzaa gift this year, I would like something
   small, like a small sports car!

This year for our Kwanzaa feast I am putting up a sign
   reading RESTAURANT CLOSED FOR HOLIDAY!

Though Kwanzaa means "first fruits," I assume you would
   like more on the table than apples and oranges

As we gather together on this happy occasion, I get to keep
   the TV remote!

Don't forget to keep the cat away from the lit kinara

One thing for certain, no gifts of fruitcake for Kwanzaa!

New Year

10 . . . 9 . . . 8 . . . 7 . . . 6 . . . Those are the heart-pounding numbers we hear counted down every December 31! As the dazzling ball descends in New York's Times Square, all across the nation noisemakers blare, fireworks explode, champagne corks pop, and kisses are exchanged, all to the familiar refrain of "Auld Lang Syne."

The celebration of the New Year is the oldest holiday in the world. But did you know that January 1 was not always the day celebrated as the beginning of the new year? The New Year was first celebrated four thousand years ago by the Babylonians, who began the year with the first new moon (the first visible crescent) after the vernal equinox, the first day of spring. It was a celebration of the beginning of the season of rebirth and planting of new crops, and it lasted for eleven days.

The Romans continued to celebrate the new year in late March, but various emperors kept changing the Roman calendar. Finally, in 153 B.C.E., the Roman senate fixed the new year to fall on January 1, as illogical and unconnected to the seasons and cycles of agriculture as that date may seem. But tampering with the calendar still continued until, in 46 B.C.E., Julius Caesar again declared January 1 to be the first day of the year.

Although the Romans continued to celebrate the new year in the first centuries C.E., the early Christian church condemned the holiday festivities as paganism. Church opposition to New Year festivities continued through the Middle

Ages, and it has only been for the past four hundred years that January 1 has been celebrated by Western nations as the beginning of the new year.

New Year Traditions

Perhaps the most popular New Year tradition is the making of New Year resolutions—those familiar promises to ourselves that we make (and so quickly break!) to lose weight and stop smoking. This tradition, too, dates back to the Babylonians—although their most popular resolution was to return borrowed farm equipment.

Another popular tradition today is the watching of the Rose Bowl parade and football game with family and friends. The Tournament of Roses Parade was first held in 1886, to celebrate the ripening of the orange crop in California. After 1916, the Rose Bowl football game was added as the centerpiece of the festival.

And the tradition of using a baby to signify the New Year? We have the Greeks to thank for that. It was their tradition around 600 B.C.E. to celebrate the wine god, Dionysius—their god of fertility—by parading a baby in a basket. The early Christians denounced the ritual as pagan, but the use of a baby as the symbol of rebirth was so popular that the Church finally relented. The depiction of a baby wearing a New Year's banner came to America with the early German immigrants, who'd been using the image since the fourteenth century.

"Should auld acquaintance be forgot . . ." In virtually every English-speaking country in the world today, these words, the opening line of the song "Auld Lang Syne," are the first we hear at the stroke of midnight as the new year begins. An old Scotch tune, at least partially written by Robert Burns and first published in 1796, "Auld Lang Syne" literally translates as "old long ago"; it simply means "the good old days."

And would New Year's Eve celebrations be complete today without the lowering of the world-famous New Year's

Eve ball from the flagpole atop One Times Square in the symbolic center of New York City? In 1904—the year the neon light was invented and the first subway was introduced in New York City—the first celebration of New Year's Eve in Times Square took place.

Until 1904, Times Square had been known as Longacre Square. On New Year's Eve of that year, then-owner of the *New York Times,* Adolph Ochs, threw a huge celebration to launch the new headquarters of his newspaper at the Times Tower, located on a tiny triangle of land at the intersection of Seventh Avenue, Broadway, and Forty-second Street. The launch became an all-day festival in the streets surrounding the Times Tower, complete with fireworks, rattles, noise-makers, and a cheering crowd of 200,000 people. The night was a rousing success, the square was renamed Times Square in honor of the paper, and a new tradition was born.

A few years later, when the city banned the fireworks display, Ochs came up with a creative solution: he arranged to have a seven-hundred-pound iron-and-wood ball, illuminated with one hundred twenty-five-watt lightbulbs, lowered from a flagpole atop the Times Tower at exactly midnight to signal the end of 1907 and the beginning of 1908.

Since then, the only time the ball has not been lit was in 1942 and 1943, due to the wartime dimout.

Today, New Year's Eve in Times Square is an international phenomenon. Hundreds of thousands of people gather around the Times Tower, now known as One Times Square, and stand for hours in the cold of a New York winter, waiting for the lowering of the famous ball. And thanks to satellite technology, billions of people around the world also watch the ball drop—an astonishing moment of global unity in welcoming the new year.

New Year Phrases

May the fireworks on this New Year's Eve start your year off with a bang!

Sending wishes for a peaceful and Happy New Year

Sending Happy New Year wishes from our home to yours

Sending the gift of love to start the New Year right

May this New Year find you healthy and happy

Hoping this New Year fulfills all your wishes and dreams

Special joy to you during the New Year holiday and always

Put on the funny hat, blow your noisemaker, and have a
   very Happy New Year!

May your New Year be happy, healthy, and prosperous

Wishing you a Happy New Year and all things bright and
   beautiful

Hoping you and those near and dear to you have a very
Happy New Year

Thinking of many past New Year celebrations and wishing
we could be with you this year

Sending warm New Year wishes to you and yours

Thinking of you during this New Year holiday and always

Wishing you love and laughter during this Happy New Year
holiday

Sending Happy New Year greetings and thinking of you often

May the New Year bring you all the happiness and joy you
so richly deserve

Hoping this New Year brings back many happy memories

Happy New Year to very special people in my life

May all your hopes and dreams come true during this
coming New Year

May your home be blessed with all that is good during this
Happy New Year

May love, hope, and happiness be yours at New Year and all
through the year

Happy New Year to our dearest friends

Wishing you the best of everything in the New Year

May all the joys of the New Year light up your heart

Hoping your New Year celebration is the start of a
wonderful year

Thinking of past New Year celebrations and all the joys we shared

May the New Year be the beginning of everything beautiful for you and your loved ones

There is no place like home for the holiday season

New Year is the perfect time to remember special neighbors

May your New Year be full of friends, family, and fun

Missing you and sending warm regards for a very Happy New Year

May your New Year celebration be the perfect finishing touch to a great year, and the start of an even better one

May the New Year bring you all you wish for and turn the
past year into happy memories

Hoping the New Year inspires you to even greater
accomplishments

May all your New Year resolutions be fulfilled

Sending wholehearted wishes for the best year yet

As you reflect on the past year, may it bring you peace and
comfort

As you gather together for this New Year celebration, our
thoughts will be with you

May you have a perfectly Happy New Year

Sending you greetings on this wonderful New Year

Sending love and affection at New Year and always

With sincere wishes for a very Happy New Year

Again and again my thoughts go back to our previous New
    Year celebrations, and it brings back much joy

Sending best regards for a very Happy New Year

Have a sparkling New Year

May your New Year be full of delights

May you have a happy and harmonious New Year

Hoping your New Year is a marvelous one

May your New Year be simply grand

May you have the finest New Year yet

May your hopes and dreams flourish in the New Year

Sending boundless wishes for a Happy New Year

May you have an abundance of good fortune in the New Year

Hoping you have an unforgettable New Year

Hoping this New Year leaves you with many sweet memories

Have a dazzling New Year celebration

Hoping you have an exceptional New Year

May the magic of the New Year holiday be with you all year

Wishing you much to look forward to during the New Year

May the New Year be filled with many joys

May good fortune smile down upon you all year

Have a super time as the ball drops!

May you receive many special blessings during the New Year

Hope you have a fun-filled New Year celebration

Sending a big hug over the miles at New Year

Wishing you peace, joy, and happiness all through the New Year

We will be thinking of you on New Year as always

Love to you at New Year and always

Thanks for all the happy memories of previous New Year
celebrations

Reaching out across the miles to wish you a very Happy
New Year

You are close to my heart at the New Year and always

Wishing a one-in-a-million friend a very Happy New Year

Sending warm and loving thoughts at the New Year and
always

🌿 New Year Humor 🌿

This year, make a resolution that you can keep: Resolve to gain twenty pounds!

I'm going to stay up until at least 9 P.M. this year and tape the ball-drop again.

Be careful when you kiss at midnight. You could wind up kissing your own husband.

One of the great things about New Year is that there are no pine needles to clean up.

What other holiday is there where you can put on a silly hat, act like an idiot, blow noisemakers, and not look stupid?

New Year is the perfect time to make promises that you know you'll never keep!

New Year's Day is such fun: women get to cook and clean up, while men get to sit and watch football!

I know it's only New Year's Day, but what are you doing next New Year's Eve?

I'm glad I'm not on the cleanup committee for Times Square after New Year's!

I resolve to keep all the resolutions I made last year and broke.

I am revolting against New Year resolutions this year!

Not to put a damper on your New Year's celebration, but remember you'll be another year older this year.

I resolve never to send another pass-on email this year.

No New Year's Eve date this year . . . guess I'll just go eat worms!

I could never figure out why I think of you every New Year's Eve. Maybe it's the size of the descending ball!

It's that time of year again—when you can act like an idiot and no one will notice!

As the New Year dawns, I hope you wake up in the right house this year!

Giving up sauerkraut isn't exactly a meaningful resolution.

I hope I meet the man of my dreams this year. They were all nightmares last year.

My New Year resolution is to give up housework, although my family believes I gave that up years ago!

Okay, who cut up the comic section to make confetti?

Reach for the stars during this New Year, but don't trip and fall!

Be careful on New Year's Eve. You know what they say . . . New Year, new baby!

Ring out the old, ring in the new, but meanwhile behave yourself!

I am making a resolution to give up gambling for the New Year. How much do you want to bet I can do it?

Famous New Year Quotations

No one ever regarded the First of
    January with indifference. It is from
    which all date their time, and count
    upon what is left. It is the nativity of
    our common Adam.

—Charles Lamb

Be at war with your vices, at peace with
    your neighbors, and let every new
    year find you a better man.

—Benjamin Franklin

Praising what is lost
Makes the remembrance dear.

—William Shakespeare

Each age has deemed the new-born year
The fittest time for festal cheer.

—Sir Walter Scott

Yesterday, everybody smoked his last
   cigar, took his last drink and swore his
   last oath. Today we are a pious and
   exemplary community. Thirty days
   from now, we shall have cast our
   reformation to the winds and gone to
   cutting our ancient shortcomings
   considerably shorter than ever.

—Mark Twain

No hand can make the clock strike for
   me the hours that are passed.

—George Gordon, Lord Byron

We meet today
To thank Thee for the era done,
And Thee for the opening one.

—John Greenleaf Whittier

The merry year is born
Like the bright berry from the naked
thorn.

—Hartley Coleridge

Ring out the old, ring in the new,
Ring, happy bells, across the snow:
The year is going, let him go;
Ring out the false, ring in the true.

—Alfred, Lord Tennyson

New Year's Day is every man's birthday

—Charles Lamb

Every man should be born again on the
    first day of January. Start with a fresh
    page. Take up one hole more in the
    buckle if necessary, or let down one,
    according to circumstances; but on the
    first of January let every man gird
    himself once more, with his face to
    the front, and take no interest in the
    things that were and are past.
                            —Henry Ward Beecher

A merry Christmas to everybody! A
    happy New Year to all the world!
                            —Charles Dickens

The new year begins in a snow-storm of
    white vows.
                            —George William Curtis

Every man regards his own life as the
New Year's Eve of time.
                              —Jean Paul Richter

Words of Sympathy during the Holidays

Though the holidays are a joyous time for most, there are circumstances that can make them difficult or sad for some. What do we write to our friends and family who are suffering through an illness, the death of a loved one, or the loss of a job?

We want to make our friend, or aunt, or sister aware that

we haven't forgotten them, but at the same time, it would be insensitive to wish them a "Happy Holiday" or send them a cheery family newsletter.

Do send a card, but with a phrase appropriate for such a difficult time.

Phrases of Sympathy

Our thoughts are with you during the holidays and always

God be with you now and always

Sending comforting thoughts during this holiday season

My heart is reaching out to you in prayer during the holidays

Though the holidays are a difficult time, please know that we are as close as a phone call

Sending warm thoughts during this difficult holiday
  season

May warm memories be a source of comfort during the
  holidays

Please know that we are here for you during the holidays
  and always

Sometimes things are easier to bear when you know friends
  care

May time and love bring you peace during the holidays and
  always

Caring thoughts are with you during the holidays

Knowing friends and family are with you hopefully makes
  your loss [illness, etc.] easier to bear

Hoping you find consolation during this holiday season, knowing that friends care

May God's love give you strength during this holiday season

You're in my thoughts and prayers during the holidays and always

Faith is a powerful force and will guide you through this holiday season

Holiday Photo-Cards

"Smile and say *cheeeeese!*"

A picture is worth a thousand words, so why not send a holiday photo-card? Show everyone how your family has grown and changed since last year! With either a digital or regular photo, you can easily create your own unique greeting card, holiday invitation card, or thank-you note.

You can take your photo to a shop and have a professional

design your card, or you can design your own card via a photo-card website. Just enter the key words *photo card* in the search engine of your web browser and you'll be given photo-card website addresses. These websites will walk you through the process of uploading your photo, editing it, and choosing a themed holiday border. You'll have the option of creating a postcard-style card or a two-page, folded card to which you'll add your personalized greeting in the font-type and color of your choice.

If you're in a particularly creative mood, try tailoring your greeting to tie into the photograph. For example, if you're using a picture of your family taken on your last vacation to Disneyland, you might write "Happy Holidays from the Smiths and Goofy!" If you're first-time parents and you're sending a photo of your new addition, try writing your holiday greeting from your child's eyes (see the holiday "kids' greetings" listed below). And don't forget the family pet! You could let Rover or Foofie do the honors of writing the greeting.

Feel free to adapt any of the phrases in the following lists or previous holiday lists to fit either a one-page photo-card or a two-page folded card.

❧ *Photo–Card Phrases* ❧

We've decked our halls, donned our gay apparel, and are sending jolly holiday greetings from our family to yours.

Silent night . . . Who are we kidding, in this house? HAPPY HOLIDAYS!

(warm weather photo) Dashing through the snow isn't all it's cracked up to be. Our warmest wishes for a happy holiday season.

(warm weather photo) We dreamed of a white Christmas but ended up on the beach—go figure! Stay warm and have the best holidays.

(face of card) Don't you just love going caroling? We sure do.
(inside of card) But this year our gift to everyone is to skip the singing and to indulge in the love and warmth of our family and friends! Merry Christmas and Happy New Year.

From our home to yours, may the holiday season bring you peace, love, and goodwill.

Ahhh . . . Holiday chaos! Is there anything better? Have a Happy Christmas and a Merry New Year!

Though we can't be with you this holiday season, we send our love and most heartfelt wishes for a wonderful holiday season.

Have a jolly, holly . . . or is it holly, jolly . . . whatever. Have
a great Christmas and a safe and wonderful New Year.

Stockings and ribbons and gifts . . . oh my! May your hopes
and wishes for this holiday season be just around the bend.

🌿 *Photo-Card Greetings from the Kids* 🌿

Everyone says I was naughty. Daddy said I was nice. No
wonder—I'm Daddy's little girl! Merry Christmas!

(face of card) Mommy said the sounds on the roof were
Santa's reindeer . . .
(inside of card) . . . but last time we heard that noise, a
squirrel came down the chimney! Hope your Christmas
is filled with fun surprises!

(new addition to family/first Christmas) Look! Santa came early this year. Hope your holidays are filled with wonder and joy.

(first Christmas) Did you hear about Santa? This is my first time! Merry Christmas.

(photo of two or more children) We figured if we sat here all nice and pretty, Santa would have to put us on the Nice List. Hope your holiday wishes come true.

(child wearing Santa hat) Santa's taking a vacation this year and I'm filling in. Hope this is your best Christmas ever!

We don't have a chimney, but Santa still comes! May your holidays be filled with wonder and happiness.

I wonder if my stocking is big enough . . . I've been REALLY good this year. Warmest wishes and glad tidings for happy and healthy holidays!

✍ *Photo-Card Greetings from the Family Pet* ✍

(photo of two or more pets) Okay . . . this year you knock over the tree, and I'll stash the good stuff. Happy Holidays from our family to yours.

(for very friendly pets) Finally—mistletoe! May your holidays be filled with love and laughter.

No accidents, no shoe chewing, no biting the groomer. The squeeze toy is a sure thing! Merry Christmas and Happy New Year.

(animal wearing Santa hat) I hope this hat gets me the extra large bone [catnip] this year. Hope your holidays bring peace, joy, and a couple of dreams-come-true.

✿ *Thank-You Photo-Cards* ✿

(face of card) Mommy said that Santa is the most generous
person ever.
(inside of card) I don't know about Santa, this being my
first Christmas, but you're pretty generous yourself!

Thanks so much for being so thoughtful.

(face of card) There's only one thing I would have liked
more than your gift . . .
(inside of card) . . . That's to have spent the holidays with
you. Thank you for being a gift yourself.

(self or family portrait) I thought of sending a fancy thank-
you, but I thought you might like to see how happy you
made me instead.

✒ *Photo-Card Invitations* ✎

(face of card) Eggnog—check. Fruitcake—check.
(inside of card) Now all we need is you, and our holiday
   party will be complete!

(face of card) We're ringing in the New Year with our
   family and closest friends.
(inside of card) So that means you have to be there!

Holidays just aren't the same without the ones you love.
   Please join us in celebrating at our home; it would be the
   perfect gift.

(face of card) Santa sent us a note. He said that you have a
   gift waiting under our tree.
(inside of card) Please don't make us return a gift from
   Santa; come and celebrate the holidays!

Short Photo-Card Phrases

Warm Christmas wishes from our home to yours

Merry Christmas from our family to yours

Wishing our best at Christmas and always

Christmas greetings from our motley crew

Many blessings at Christmas

Good wishes to all

Holiday Greetings

Joy to the world

Holiday Thank-You Notes

It is always appropriate to express gratitude through a thank-you note. Even if you make an appreciative phone call, writing a thank-you note adds a special touch.

Thank-you notes should be sent as quickly as possible after you've received a gift or enjoyed someone's hospitality. When a gift comes by mail, a prompt reply should especially be made to make certain the sender knows you've received the gift.

Thank-you notes do not have to be lengthy. Be brief, meaningful, and to the point. Put yourself in the gift-sender's place and imagine what you would like to read, and your words will certainly come from the heart!

When you've enjoyed a friend's or relative's hospitality, flowers with a personalized card make the perfect thank-you gift.

When you receive flowers as a gift, be sure to describe the flowers in the thank-you note, as the sender may not know what the delivered arrangement looked like.

In thanking a gift- or party-giver, note some detail. Always mention the gift or the occasion for the party, and be specific. Remark in your note how much you love the dark red color of the sweater, or the softness of the scarf. Tell your hostess how much you enjoyed that tender roast beef, or fragrant eggnog. If you recall a specific detail, then the recipient will know how important and memorable the gift or the evening was to you. For example: "Thank you so much for the beautiful sweater. Each time I wear it, I will think of you.

And it was so thoughtful of you to remember that my favorite color is blue."

When it comes to gifts of money, however, don't disclose the specific amount. Instead, a good term to use is "generous gift." You might also tell the giver that you're going to purchase something special that you've been holding off buying (and name that something), and that you will think of the giver every time you wear or use it.

Sometimes you have to be deceptively tactful. If you find a gift is not to your taste, try to be as gracious as possible. Again, put yourself in the gift-giver's place. They may have put much time and effort into this gift, and a smiling face and a brief thank-you note will make them happy. I'm certain you can find a useful purpose for the gift, and meanwhile you've strengthened a relationship.

❧ Thank-You Phrases ❧

Thank you for making our holiday so special with your
   generous hospitality

Thanks for the wonderful hat [toaster, magazine
   subscription, etc.]. Every time I wear it [use it, read it],
   I will think of you.

Your thoughtfulness during this wonderful holiday season
   meant so much to me

I was so pleased to receive your thoughtful gift of . . .

The company was perfect and the food was great. Thank
   you.

May your holiday be as happy as you've made mine

We were all so deeply touched by your thoughtfulness

Your gift was so unexpected, but deeply appreciated

How sweet of you to think of us at this hectic time of the year

Your thoughtful gift couldn't have come at a more perfect time

I can't remember when I've enjoyed myself more

I will cherish your gift always

It was so kind of you to include us in your lovely holiday dinner party

Thank you from the bottom of my heart

It was a perfect idea for a gift

Your thoughtfulness really put sunshine in my holiday

How beautiful a holiday can be when kindness touches it

So thoughtful of you to think of us during this holiday
season

You always do the nicest things in the nicest ways

Thank you for being you

Thanks for filling our holiday with fun and laughter

I can tell that much thought went into my gift and that
makes it even more special

The Family Holiday Newsletter

The winter holiday season is the perfect time to update family and friends with the highlights of your year. The family newsletter is the perfect way to do this.

The wonderful world of email enables us to keep in touch with friends and family around the country and around the world. Though this modern miracle is convenient, it cannot take the place of the family newsletter during the holidays.

While some don't approve of this tradition, others are happy to send them and thankful to receive them, as it keeps them informed about the lives of their friends and loved ones. New babies, weddings, graduations, divorces, illness, and the passing of a loved one are all part of our daily lives. It is difficult to keep friends and family informed all year long, so this is the perfect time to update them.

Here, computers do become important: they make it so much easier to type and print your newsletter! And beautiful holiday paper makes it even more festive.

Through the year, as you go about your daily routine and you think of something you would like to include in your newsletter, jot it down. Refresh your memory by going back through the year's calendar. Put all these notes in one special area—perhaps a box—so when you're ready to start your letter, you will have these notes to jump-start your thought process.

Don't put off writing the newsletter until the last minute.

Start writing in October and you'll have plenty of time to revise. (Don't be a stranger to a grammar book, and be sure to ask someone to proofread your letter when you've finished.)

Before sitting down with pen and paper, or at the computer, create an atmosphere conducive to writing. Creating a family newsletter can be an enjoyable and relaxing experience if you set the right mood.

Set aside a special time when you know you will have a peaceful house, put on your favorite holiday CD, light your favorite scented candles, pour a mug of hot chocolate or a glass of wine, dim the lights, or do whatever puts you in the right holiday mood. Allow your mind to flow back through all the meaningful things that have happened in the year.

Of course, you will start your letter with a cheerful and happy greeting, or perhaps a humorous anecdote. The main body of the letter should be pleasantly informative, but brief. One way of informing people about your family news is by writing a brief paragraph for each member of the family.

If you have the technology and know-how, include a digital photo of the family on your newsletter. Don't forget the family pet! Put Fluffy or Fido in the photo. (And if you're in an especially creative mood, write the family newsletter through your pet's eyes.)

Try to keep the happy news, such as weddings, births, new pets, etc., in the beginning of your newsletter. In this area you may be less brief and more descriptive.

Illness, divorce, the passing of a loved one, etc., should be kept quite brief. If more details are requested, it should be done at another time, either person to person or in a telephone call.

If you know the recipient of your newsletter has had a difficult time recently, skip the family newsletter. It is more considerate to write a short, thoughtful note directly on the card, rather than an upbeat account of how great *your* life has been this past year. (See the section titled "Words of Sympathy during the Holidays" for appropriate phrases.) Also, let the recipient know that you will be in personal contact with her or him after the holidays.

The closing of your letter should be happy and cheerful, wishing the recipients a wonderful holiday and a happy, healthy, and prosperous New Year.

Save space at the bottom of your newsletter for a handwritten message to each individual. A printed newsletter can seem cold and impersonal, so this personal note will put a perfect finishing touch to your newsletter.

❧ Sample Family Newsletter ❧

Happy Holidays!

Hot off the presses . . . the traditional Hoffman holiday news-letter!

Mark retired from his job last May and has since become quite the homebody. He'd been with the airlines for thirty-eight years, so retirement's been quite an adjustment. I manage to keep him busy with all the home repairs that I've been saving up for him. It's been great having him home, but I now know the meaning of the word hover!

Our daughter and son-in-law, Stacey and Tom, now happily married for twenty-one years, have just bought a new home. (They had to have a larger place to accommodate their nine cats!!)

Our granddaughter, Molly, turned ten in December. She plays soccer and is the ambassador of her fourth-grade class.

Our son, Paul, is still single but dating a great girl named Sandy, and it looks like there might be wedding bells in their future.

It's hard to believe our Irish setter, Shannon, will be three next year. He's great company, a super watchdog, and we don't mind a bit that he barks long and loud every time the phone rings!

As for me, between the housework, laundry, keeping up with the family, taking care of the dog, and babysitting, I rarely have time for myself—except for reading, going to the casino, getting my hair done, and going to exercise class! So what did I do this year? I got a part-time job at a gift store! I really love it, and it gets me out of the house, unhovered!

We were finally able to get away this year. Mark and I went to Denver, where we stopped at Lookout Mountain and toured Buffalo Bill Cody's gravesite and museum. Mark thinks he looks like Buffalo Bill in his ten-gallon hat, and who am I to say he doesn't?

As far as our health goes, we've been fairly healthy this year except for a few colds and a couple of bouts with the flu.

My dad was in the hospital earlier this year with pneumonia. Thank heavens it was a slight case, and he was home quickly and is now extremely healthy. Pretty good for someone who's ninety-seven!

I can hardly believe Christmas is almost here. I've been having a great time decorating the house, shopping, wrapping, and planning for the holidays. I really love Christmas!

We think of you often and hope you're well and happy during this wonderful holiday season.

Wishing you a very Merry Christmas and all the best in the New Year!

Helpful Hints to Simplify Holiday Card-Sending

Do you put off writing your holiday cards until the last minute? Do you find every excuse not to start?

Holiday card-sending always seems to be a chore, but it doesn't have to be that way. It can be an enjoyable opportunity to connect with friends and family. All it takes is a little organization, breaking it down into small jobs and starting early.

There are some things you can do at any time of the year to prepare yourself for holiday card-writing. Gather everything you need for writing your cards in one container: address book, cards, newsletters, pens, stamps, return-address labels, stickers, etc. Once you've created this card-writing box, you'll have it at your fingertips year-round. Keep it within easy reach.

In October, update your holiday card list, adding or deleting names and updating addresses. Or if you have created your holiday card box, you can continually update your card list all year. And if you are going to create a family newsletter, you've been jotting notes down throughout the year and putting them into your holiday card-writing box.

Anytime after Thanksgiving is a good time to start writing out the cards. If you start early, you will only need to write a few cards each day, say five or ten at a sitting. You'll find it much less tedious if you spread them out.

Address all the envelopes first, but do not seal any of the envelopes until just before mailing. That makes it much easier to change or add something to the card, or to include the family newsletter. Do the cards that require a short personal note first. Save the cards you wish to write longer personal messages on for last.

As you receive cards, add friends or family members who've sent you a card to your recipient lists, if they're not already on it, and send them a card. Even after the holidays, it's never too late to send a New Year's greeting.

An important part of card writing is creating the right mood. A peaceful house is a great start. Next, put on your favorite holiday CD, light your favorite scented candles, and treat yourself to some hot chocolate or a glass of wine. Happy card-sending!

🌿 State Abbreviations 🌿

Alabama-AL

Alaska-AK

Arizona-AZ

Arkansas-AR

California-CA

Colorado-CO

Connecticut-CT

Delaware-DE

District of Columbia-DC

Florida-FL

Georgia-GA

Hawaii-HI

Idaho-ID

Illinois-IL

Indiana-IN

Iowa-IA

Kansas-KS

Kentucky-KY

Louisiana-LA

Maine-ME

Maryland-MD

Massachusetts-MA

Michigan-MI

Minnesota-MN

Mississippi-MS

Missouri-MO

Montana-MT

Nebraska-NE

Nevada-NV

New Hampshire-NH

New Jersey-NJ

New Mexico-NM

New York-NY

North Carolina-NC

North Dakota-ND

Ohio-OH

Oklahoma-OK

Oregon-OR

Pennsylvania-PA

Rhode Island-RI

South Carolina-SC

South Dakota-SD

Tennessee-TN

Texas-TX

Utah-UT

Vermont-VT

Virginia-VA

Washington-WA

West Virginia-WV

Wisconsin-WI

Wyoming-WY

Holiday Card Recipient Lists

Christmas

Hanukkah

Kwanzaa

New Year

....

....

....

....

....

....

....

....

....

....

....

....

....